Successfully Defending (And Winning) DUI Cases In Virginia

Don't Be A Victim... Fight Back

By O. Keith Hallam, Jr., Esq.

ISBN: 978-1-941645-25-3

Design and Published by:

Speakeasy Publications

73-03 Bell Blvd #10

Oakland Gardens, N.Y. 11364

www.SpeakeasyMarketingInc.com

888-225-8594

DISCLAIMER

This publication is intended to be informational only. No legal advice is being given, and no attorney-client relationship is intended to be created by reading this material. If you are facing legal issues, whether criminal or civil, seek professional legal counsel to get your questions answered.

NovaLegalGroup, P.C.

1507 King Street

Alexandria, VA 22314

(703) 548-1462

www.NovaLegalGroup.com

CLIENT TESTIMONIALS

"Mr. Hallam is a superb lawyer. He did a great job for me which resulted in a good result. He is passionate about his work and clients and strives to achieve the best result. In addition to being a high caliber professional, he is compassionate and takes a personal interest in the case." **- Teji**

"I am more than grateful that Mr. Hallam and his colleagues were able to help me with my case. I was facing a DUI with a BAC greater than .20, and I was involved in an accident. He fought for me and had my back the whole way. When it came down to my trial everything was dismissed by the grace of God, I am truly blessed. I recently recommended one of my friends to his office. Im for certain that he will fight for them the same way he fought for me. He let me know the brutal truth about my case and didnt give me false hope. I will forever be thankful for what Mr. Hallam did for me. And I will always recommend him to anyone who is looking for an attorney. Thank you all so much for all of your help, I am beyond grateful." **- Diamond**

"Mr. Hallam helped me out of what could have been a very bad situation for my record, future job prospects, etc. He and his office are very reliable."

- A Criminal Defense Client

....

"Wanted to express how amazing my treatment was with Keith and his associates. He jumped on my case immediately. Got things resolved very affordably and in a timely manner with out the run around I have received with prior counsel. Followed up with me after my court date which I felt was wonderful. Keith and his team are proffession, prompt, and worked quickly to resolve my case. I would highly recommend Keith for your next attorney. Everything from the person receiveing the calls to returning my calls was handle professionally. I would definitely choose Keith again in the future." **- Todd**

....

TABLE OF CONTENTS

ABOUT THE AUTHOR

O. Keith Hallam, Jr. has practiced Criminal Traffic Law, Criminal Law and Personal Injury/Accident Law for nearly 30 years – successfully representing over 10,000+ clients during this time, throughout all the courts of Northern Virginia and many other courts throughout all of Virginia. Mr. Hallam is well-known throughout this area as being one of the first, if not the first attorney, to design customized "Plans of Action" for he and his clients to pursue together, requiring that both he and his clients work as a "team," together to successfully defend and win their cases.

Mr. Hallam's customized "Plans of Action" are designed so that both the attorney and the client have well-defined, due diligence actions and "homework" to perform proactively before court, so as to determine and find "holes" in the prosecution's case and for the client to engage in certain actions and take certain classes before court, such as various "Driver Improvement" classes; alcohol education classes; community service and letters of recommendations, all to place the client in the most favorable light possible when the attorney must try the DUI case or work to negotiate a favorable reduction or dismissal of the DUI charge with the prosecutor.

Mr. Hallam has also been one of the first attorneys in Northern Virginia to put trust and confidence in his clients, as they do him by designing customized "Payment Plans" to fit each client's unique financial situation.

SUCCESSFULLY DEFENDING (AND WINNING) DUI CASES IN VIRGINIA!

Don't Be A Victim..... Fight Back!

Why Do Some People Call Drunk Driving Charges A "DWI" And Others A "DUI"? Are They The Same, Or Not?

The terms "DWI and DUI" are often used interchangeably, but, in Virginia, there is a significant difference between the terms "DWI and DUI". A DWI is a drunk driving charge in which the person charged has either blown a 0.08%Blood Alcohol Concentration (BAC), or higher, or has actually had their blood drawn by a specially trained technician and analyzed by Virginia's Division of Forensic Science, and is also 0.08% BAC, or higher. In Virginia, a 0.08% BAC, or higher, means the person is presumed to be legally intoxicated.

For reference, a 0.00% BAC means that there is <u>no</u> alcohol in their system whereas a 0.30% BAC means that the person is in immediate danger of alcohol poisoning, likely coma and death.

When a person refuses to take a breath test at the police station or a blood test at the station, or is involved in other Breath or Blood test failure scenarios, the person will be charged with both "DUI" and "Unreasonable Refusal" to take a breath or blood test.

Therefore, a "DUI" technically means that there is no breath or blood test result that can be used against the person in Court to prove drunk driving; but the Police and Prosecutor believe that they can still prove the person guilty of "Drunk Driving" by the way the person looks, acts, walks (unsteady gait/stumbling), talks (slurred speech) and does on the roadside "Field Sobriety Tests", etc.

Both a DWI and DUI carry the same penalties: a Class 1 Misdemeanor Criminal Record with the FBI, Homeland Security, NCIS, Immigration and all Court and Police departments nationally for the rest of their life; up to 1 year in jail; up to a $2,500 fine (or both); mandatory loss of driver's license privilege for 1 year; a mandatory "Ignition Interlock " device that must be paid for and have installed in your car for at least 6 months; mandatory Alcohol Safety Action Program (ASAP) classes; 6 negative demerit points on their DMV record; and obtaining high- risk/ higher premium auto insurance for a significant period of time.

**Please note: From here on, for the sake of brevity and clarity, I will refer to any "Drunk Driving" charge as a "DUI", as all of the penalties for both charges are exactly the same.*

WHY DO YOU DEFEND DUI CASES?

The primary reason I have chosen to defend DUI cases is truly because everyone is presumed innocent unless and until either they have been found guilty by a judge or jury; or, if they have pleaded "Guilty" or "No Contest" to the charge; even if their Breath or Blood BAC is 0.08% or higher and they are "legally " and practically drunk.

The second reason is because if a person is found guilty of a DUI in Virginia, they face a nightmare of problems and penalties that will severely damage or destroy the "American Dream" for the rest of their life. The penalties including up to a year in jail; mandatory loss of their driver's license for one year; mandatory Alcohol Safety Action Program classes for several months; paying a fine up to a $2,500 plus Court Costs; paying to have installed and rent an "Ignition Interlock" device in their car for a mandatory minimum of 6 months if they qualify for a Restricted Driver's License for work, school, doctors, etc. (with absolutely no stopping to get gas for their car, no trips to the grocery store or drug store to buy food or medicine for themselves or their family, etc. They will also receive 6 negative points on their DMV record and be required to obtain very expensive "High Risk" auto insurance.

Clearly, these are terrible personal, work and social consequences, right? But, believe it or not, there are even worse consequences that most people don't even know about. If you want to know what they are then read on at your own peril!

A DUI is not a "Traffic" charge, even though it involves a car and is indeed handled in Virginia's "Traffic Courts"- rather, it is actually a serious "Class One (1) Criminal Misdemeanor" charge , Virginia's highest and most serious Misdemeanor. What this means for you is that if you plead guilty or no contest to a DUI Charge, (or are found guilty by a Judge), even if you are not sentenced to jail, you will have a Class 1 Criminal Misdemeanor on your Permanent Lifetime Criminal Record on the National Crime Information Center (NCIC) database; where all criminal conviction

records are maintained and integrated with the FBI, Homeland Security, Immigration and all local and national court, law enforcement, and intelligence agency records for the rest of your life.

What are the results on your life if you have a Class 1 Misdemeanor Criminal Record? You will almost certainly lose any security clearance you now have, (or never will get if ever applied for). Very possibly you may lose your job (and likely never get the job or career you have been working so hard for). Most likely you will never be able to be accepted as a "Volunteer Coach" or "Team Parent" at your kid's school or local sports teams.

Also, this Criminal Record is also a "Public" Criminal Record, available to anyone who wants to check you out on the Internet; including your family, your neighbors, your friends and your employers, who will always then see you in a "different light".

Should Someone Consider Representing Themselves?

As noted previously, Shakespeare said it best in one of his Plays, "He or she who represents themselves, has a Fool for a client and an Ass for an attorney". This quote, that we often give to potential clients, drives home the message to most people. I then ask them how would they be able to represent themselves when they are

both emotionally involved, and trying to defend themselves, all at the same time.

I also show them that they simply do not know the law and do not know Court procedures, as there is no reason for them to know. I tell them that they might as well just go in to Court, plead guilty, and get it over with-rather than going through the "drama and trauma" of trying to represent themselves; because representing themselves is bound to be an even bigger disaster.

I tell them that they need to get an experienced DUI Defense Attorney, and I tell them that even if they do not want to hire me, that they should hire someone who is experienced in handling at least hundreds, if not thousands, of DUI cases over many years in Northern Virginia Courts. I urge everyone to get the best representation possible, especially ours!

WHAT DO YOU THINK ABOUT PUBLIC DEFENDERS?

Public Defenders are good attorneys and they mean well. We have all passed the same Bar Exam to become lawyers. But, the biggest difference between a retained/private attorney and a Public Defender is that Public Defenders are almost always overworked and underpaid. They are often young lawyers who want to get some legal experience, then move into private practice.

Even if a Public Defender has been there a long time, they are still overworked and often are forced by work and time constraints, to ask their clients to come in for short meetings; or even just meet them, for the first time, in court, often with no time for much else.

They are dedicated, hard-working, and mean well; but they just do not have the time to focus, in-depth, on any one person's case, the way a private/retained attorney can.

Why Do People Feel So "Doomed" That They Might Not Want To Talk To An Attorney?

First, most people do have a sense of guilt or remorse about their DUI charge-because they know they were drinking, or consuming drugs, or both, and driving. Most people instinctively know that from the legal perspective, they are likely "guilty as charged" of a DUI.

They know in their hearts that they probably drank too much that night, and were possibly over the legal limit of 0.08% BAC. They usually know that they at least had a "Buzz". They are also often "Beating themselves up"; scared and confused-afraid they may lose their job, their house and their family.

People are often ashamed and embarrassed, and don't want anyone to know they were charged with a DUI. They certainly don't want their bosses to know; and often don't even want their friends or spouses to know either. They are afraid of what this will do to their career, and afraid of having a Permanent Criminal Record for the rest of their life. By the time the person calls an attorney, their head is spinning. They're worried about everything. They might have heard stories from friends who had DUIs, and they probably have gone on the Internet and read DUI "horror" stories; so they get confused with too much information and misinformation.

Do Some People Just Want To "Give Up" Because They Are Charged With A DUI?

Sure, many people call me feeling as if there is nothing anybody can do for them. Maybe they have called me only because their family, a spouse or a friend insisted that they talk to a lawyer. They often feel this way because they know that the Commonwealth of Virginia has all of its resources, (the Police, the Prosecutors and much of the law), working against them. They just feel like they don't have a chance. But, this is not true!

Everybody charged with a DUI can be helped and my office has successfully handled more than One Thousand DUI cases over nearly 30 years; and there isn't a single DUI case that I can think of that we have handled where we weren't able to do something positive to make the outcome of the case better for our client than it was when they first picked up the phone to call and talk to us. When they do talk to us, we show them how to change their whole perspective on their case; get them "pumped- up" and excited to help us to help them in defending and attacking their DUI charge. In essence we will tell them, *"Don't Be A Victim... Fight Back!... We'll Show You How!"*

How Can An Attorney Help The Client Feel Better?

People come to us with having received bad advice and misinformation, and want to know what can be done about their situation and how an attorney can help deal with it. It's the attorney's job to provide them with the correct information and a customized "Plan of Action"; so that when the potential client is done talking with us, they will be more informed, more optimistic and more hopeful for a positive outcome.

People feel much more comfortable when they have a customized "Plan of Action" and are <u>involved</u> in their own defense. Some attorneys say they will "take care" of the client; but then <u>just</u> show up in court without really preparing or caring. It makes a big difference when an attorney really cares about the client; knows about them personally; and then creates a customized "Plan of Action" for them. Once they have a customized "Plan of Action" in place, then they are in a very different emotional and mental condition than when they first talked to us – a much better condition!

What Special Do You Do For Your Clients That Makes You Stand Out From Other Attorneys?

First, we get as much information as possible about the client, their life, their job, their family and, of course, the facts of their DUI case. The first contact we have with virtually every client is

by their first telephone call to our office. It is our strict office policy that either myself, or one of my "Team" of experienced DUI attorneys, will always speak, at length, with every potential client who calls us seeking help and advice on their first call!

In fact, our policy is that we will always talk with you on the phone for as long as you need and want to talk with us about your DUI charge; the law; how to handle the specific DUI Criminal charge you are facing and, most importantly, explore the ways we can work together to get your DUI charge dismissed, (or at least reduced to a minor traffic charge) by using our knowledge and experience from handling more than One Thousand DUI's over nearly 30 years.

People are always amazed that attorneys, like us, will actually get on the phone and spend 45 minutes, one hour, or more with them, even before they come in for their first Free in-person Consultation. Many people wonder why we do this. They think we must lose a lot of time and money this way. But, they are wrong! Spending this kind of time on the first call allows us to build a bond of trust, confidence and a "connection" together. It also gives us the opportunity to get as much information as possible to help them with their DUI case. We invest our time and effort in our clients, even before they hire us; and, in turn, they invest their trust and confidence in us.

Most of the potential clients we speak with on the telephone also come in for a personal, one-on-one, in-depth Free Consultation with myself, or one of my experienced DUI Criminal attorney's-so that we can go over the detailed facts of their case; explain how DUI law works; and, how it applies to them; and then we discuss a specific customized "Plan of Action" for them to deal with the "DUI", (and any other charges they also might have incurred). This is just the beginning of the process of our office representing and helping someone with a DUI.

After we gather all this information from the potential client, we then tell them the details of the DUI law they are charged with and the Court's detailed procedures. Then, we begin the process of giving them the outline of a Customized Defense "Plan of Action" to show them how we can help them get the criminal "DUI" charge dismissed, or at least reduced to a lesser traffic- related charge; or reduce and minimize the various penalties that they face with a DUI charge. We also quote every potential client a reasonable fee; explain it, in depth; and, if they need it, we offer every potential client a Customized Payment Plan to fit their financial situations.

All of the above is just what we do on the first telephone call. We then invite all potential Clients in for a one-on-one appointment with myself, or with one of our "Team" of experienced and successful DUI attorneys at "NovaLegalGroup, P.C." - where we genuinely get to know one another in order to finalize our Customized "Plan of Action" and to further build trust and confidence in one another.

Do Clients Feel Differently At The End Of The First Phone Call Than They Did At The Beginning?

Yes! Absolutely! Many of the potential clients we speak with on the phone have often already talked to several other attorneys, and they often tell us that their needs have <u>not</u> been met by the other attorneys they have talked to. This is often typically why they have called me. It's a very good thing, when people are facing a DUI charge, to do their own due diligence; and it's a good idea for them to talk with several attorneys. But, over and over again, I hear from these potential clients that no other attorney has spent as much time with them as myself and my experienced "Team" of "DUI" attorneys do.

Many of these potential clients tell us that most of these other attorneys just tell them to "come in" and won't even talk with them on the phone; or will only talk very briefly, then quote them a Fee-usually telling the potential client that they must pay <u>all</u> of their Attorney's Fee <u>upfront</u> or, at the least, pay one- half of their Fee upfront, and the other half before their first Court date. Or, they charge such a low fee that it makes them think that these are "Bottom Feeders" who just want to "Bleed and Plead" them. Then, they are very happy with us because we've cared enough to take the time for an attorney to actually speak to them, in-depth, on the phone; and are very thankful for us giving them direction and a customized "Plan of Action" of how we can work together to potentially get their DUI dismissed, or reduced to a Traffic charge; and how we can give them a very reasonable fee with a customized "Payment Plan" to meet their financial need.

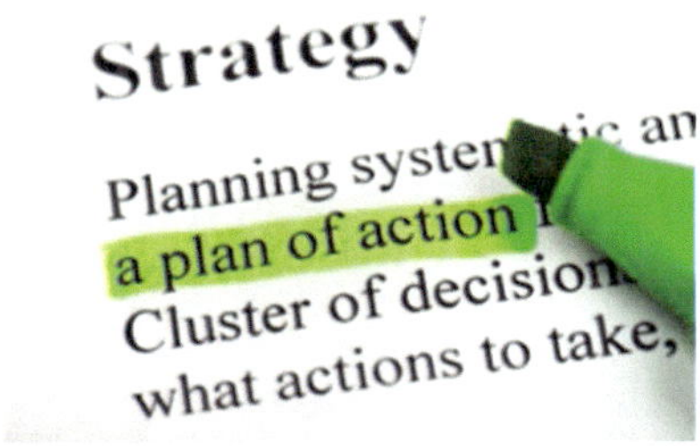

Then, when a potential client comes in to meet with us, in-person, we then get to know them even better; we go over their past driving history; what they do for a living; (do they have a Government job and/ or a "Security Clearance"); do they drive for a living (a Taxi, Limo, Bus or Uber driver); how important is their driving privilege to them; will they likely lose their job or security clearance if they get a DUI conviction; are they a U.S. Citizen, (if not, they might suffer severe Immigration consequences); what is their economic situation, their family situation, their educational background. We gather all of their personal information first, then we have them give us the details of their DUI case; were they drinking, and if so, what; how much did they have to drink-when and where; did they consume any legal or illegal drugs or medication before driving; were they on any medication (prescribed or over the counter), and, if so, what medicine and dosage; did they eat anything before or while drinking- if so, what did they eat and when?

After gathering all of this information, and more, we then ask the potential client what happened on the road; and why was the vehicle they were driving "pulled over"? What, if anything, did they admit to having had to drink or drugs consumed? What roadside "Field Sobriety Test" (FST's) did they do and how do they believe they did on each of the usual FST's [9 step/ heel-toe/ walk and turn test; standing on one leg test; counting 1-4/ 4-1 on each finger to thumb; counting backwards (65- 35); saying a portion of the alphabet, e.g. D-R; Horizontal Gaze Nystagmus Eye test (following a pen or penlight with their eyes as the officer moves the pen/penlight sideways/ up and down, without moving your head].

We then ask them about the roadside Breath test known as the "Preliminary Breath Test" (PBT) that is not admissible in Court as evidence of "DUI" guilt; but, is a FST test, along with all of the other roadside FST's; as well as their driving behavior; admission of any drinking; answers to Police questions; the way they looked and acted, all of which is used by the Police Officer to determine whether or not there was "Probable Cause" (whether it is more likely than not that they might be drunk driving), to arrest them for DUI.

If the Police Officer believes there is "Probable Cause" to arrest the person, then they are arrested and taken to the Police Station, where they are read Virginia's "Implied Consent Law", (A law that states that every person who is driving on a Virginia road has already impliedly given their consent to take a Breath Test or Blood Test if the arresting Officer reasonably believes that they may be driving under the influence of alcohol). The Police, at the station, must then conduct a "20 minute" wait/observation period during which they are instructed to not belch, burp, spit or get sick within the "20 minute" wait period, (because it would alter the Breath Test Result). If they do burp, belch, etc., then the 20 minute wait/observation period will be repeated again.

If they are not successful in providing a valid Breath Test analysis, a second time they "blow", then they will be charged with both DUI and "Unreasonable Refusal" to take the Breath Test; for which they might not only be convicted of the DUI, but also convicted of "Unreasonable Refusal" to take a Breath Test (resulting in the person losing their privilege to drive for a mandatory period of one year- without the possibility of obtaining any kind of "Restricted Driving" privilege to drive to work, to the doctor, or anything else).

So You Have A Plan Of Action For The Client Before They Even Come In?

Absolutely! That is what sets us apart from virtually all other attorneys. We do not get off the phone on any potential Client's first call to us until we've gathered information regarding their life; their DUI charge; and the facts of their case. Then we give them a customized "Plan of Action" for us to discuss, more in-depth, when they come in to meet with us, in person.

When we do meet with them, we begin to put that customized "Plan of Action" into effect to successfully defend them against their DUI charge.

WHAT IS THE BENEFIT OF OUR LAW FIRM PREPARING A CUSTOMIZED "PLAN OF ACTION" FOR THE CLIENT; AND THE CLIENT BEING PROACTIVE?

Despite the significant amount of "Due Diligence" we do, we cannot always rely on finding something wrong with the police case against our clients. For most Client's , this is a first time, life-altering event- for the Police Officer, this is just another routine DUI arrest-all in a night's work.

Therefore, we ask our clients to also use "due diligence" and be <u>proactive</u> with us. We help prepare their defense and usually continue their Court date into the future as far as we can to give them time to take an 8-Hour "Virginia Driver Improvement" Class <u>before</u> we go to court. By doing this, they get 5+ points on their Virginia Driving Record and, in Court, it looks very positive to the Prosecutor and to the Judge that they've re-educated themselves on Virginia driving law <u>before</u> they go to court. We also often have them take a 4-hour "Aggressive/Reckless Driving" class and, in some cases, perhaps have them enroll in ASAP classes and do 25 hours of volunteer Community Service, all before Court.

We strongly encourage nearly all of our DUI clients to do all of these proactive measures, so that when we talk with the Prosecutor, before Court, if we cannot find any errors or "holes" in the Prosecutor's case to likely win at trial, then we have a customized back- up "Plan of Action" to negotiate to get the DUI charge dismissed or reduced to a "Reckless Driving" or, perhaps, we can even get the DUI charge reduced to "Improper Driving", (a non-criminal/non-infraction minor traffic finding. I don't believe that an attorney is doing their complete job if they don't both do their legal Due Diligence, and have their Client do their own Proactive "Homework". By doing all of these things together, we give our clients a much greater chance of our either winning their case at trial, dismissed before trial, or reduced to a lesser charge/lesser penalties.

Does This Proactive "Team" Work Have A Significant Positive Effect On The Outcome Of The Case?

Yes! All of this proactive work by the clients, as part of our "Team", serves to demonstrate that the client wants to be a better driver and a better citizen. It demonstrates genuine remorse, if appropriate, without ever admitting guilt. It almost always does something to either have the DUI dismissed; reduced to a lesser charge; or, to reduce the severity of DUI penalties and punishment.

Are There Any Common Misconceptions About DUI Charges In Virginia?

People often don't know what the Blood Alcohol Concentration (BAC) number means; such as a BAC of 0.08%, or higher. This is the Blood Alcohol number the person gets if they have been consuming alcohol before they blow into a "Preliminary Breath Test" device, out on the road when they're stopped by the police; or, at the police station; or, if their blood is drawn and analyzed by a scientist at Virginia's Division of Forensic Sciences.

Most people have heard all kinds of things about DUI charges from friends, co-workers or relatives regarding a BAC number, and what it means; or how many glasses of wine, liquor or beer it takes to get to the nationwide drunk driving legal limit of 0.08% BAC. Most of what they will have heard is simply wrong! Most people usually don't have any realistic idea about how alcohol actually affects them; or how their weight, size, gender, what they have just eaten and what medicines taken will also interact with their alcohol intake. Their BAC number, and what affects it, is probably the biggest misconception about DUI's we see.

WHAT MISTAKES DO PEOPLE MAKE REGARDING DUI CASES?

Many people either think that their DUI case is hopeless, and therefore they don't think getting a lawyer can help them; or, they don't know, or appreciate, all of the terrible consequences of a DUI conviction, or, they see themselves as a smart, intelligent and successful person in their personal and professional lives (which they may very likely be) ... they believe that they can do some research on the Internet, talk to friends or relatives who have had a DUI before, or, even worse, talk to several lawyers to "pick their brains" and then think they can put all of their "research" together, and handle their DUI case themselves.

Why is this thinking one of the biggest mistakes of their life? Well, I could give you literally hundreds of reasons why (including just plain old "Common Sense") that makes thinking of representing themselves a disaster , but I will leave the answer to Shakespeare. Shakespeare said it best in one of his Plays... "He or she who represents themselves, has a FOOL for a Client, and an ASS for an Attorney".

The second major mistake almost all people make is that they are overly "Price- Conscious" about the attorney's fee they are going to have to pay. While it seems that this may be easy for me to say, since I'm an attorney, I say this for the benefit of anyone charged with a DUI-The laws surrounding a DUI are detailed and complex, with traps and dead-ends, and with numerous potential options and defense strategies to consider and pursue. There are time-sensitive deadlines that must be known and adhered to. There is their past "Driving Record" that must be reviewed. In essence, do you want the "cheapest" lawyer money can buy; or, do you want the "best" lawyer you are comfortable with for your case.

At my Law Firm, I give a fair and reasonable fee for the nearly 30 years of experience, and the more than One Thousand DUI cases we have successfully handled throughout all of the Northern Virginia Courts; and we always offer the option of a customized "Payment Plan"

paid over several months for our Standard Fee... or, a Reduced Fee if they pay the Attorney fee all upfront. What this means is that we will work with you to meet your financial needs that is fair to both of us.

A "win-win" situation for all of us!

Where Do You Find The Most Relevant Defenses For DUI Cases?

In DUI cases, and in every criminal case we handle, we first find out about the Client's social, work and family lives and obligations. Then, we get the facts of their case and explain the DUI laws to the client. We then apply the facts to the law, and the law to the facts, to see where we can find "holes" in the prosecution's case and opportunities for dismissal or reduction of the charge. Then, we develop a customized "Plan of Action" for our Clients.

We begin finding out if there were any errors in the way the police handled the traffic "stop", the Breath test, the FST's, the arrest, etc. to determine the best customized defense and "Plan of Action" for each client.

Do Social And Economic Factors Effect Who Gets A DUI?

Anyone, from any walk of life can, and does get a DUI- from Congressional and White House aides, to people in the CIA and the Defense Department; and from people who dig ditches and

haul trash, to lawyers and doctors. Whether rich or poor; whether black, white or brown; almost everyone has, at one time or another, put themselves in a potential DUI arrest scenario.

Clearly, in tough economic times there is an increase in the pressures and tensions that cause some people to drink too much; but <u>no</u> groups of people are immune from getting a DUI.

WHO GETS ARRESTED MORE OFTEN- MEN OR WOMEN?

There are significantly more men who get arrested for DUI's than women (an almost 4 to 1 ratio). There are several reasons why. Men have a special enzyme in their stomach that women do not have, that breaks down alcohol before it reaches the brain. This enzyme is like the "Pacman" character who, in the old video game, went around eating up little pellets. In addition, men are simply, much larger than women, causing alcohol to have to be spread over a larger mass than women; and, men's bodies are made up of 55%-65% water; while women's bodies are only made up of 45%-55% water.

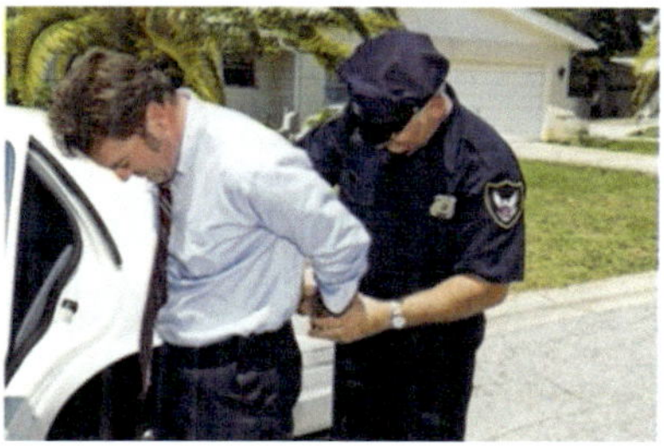

Therefore, men's bodies have more water in their system to dilute the alcohol before reaching the brain than women's bodies. Thus, it can take much longer and much more alcohol for men to reach a drunk driving level of a BAC of 0.08% than women.

Alcohol literally goes to women's heads faster and more powerfully than to men's heads. Women tend to feel the effects of alcohol much more quickly, and realize they may be getting drunk much sooner than men do. It is relatively rare to see intoxicated women driving a car because they know they are feeling drunk sooner and will likely have asked a friend or a taxi to drive them home. While there are other cultural and social factors involved, it is still overwhelmingly men who get caught and charged with a DUI.

How Can The Attorney Use Due Diligence To Help The Case?

We prepare ourselves ,and our clients, to be proactive-and then we work-together as a "Team". We obtain the records for the Breath Test machine that the client blew in to at the police station, going back two months. By doing this, we are able to look at every person who blew on that machine during the two months prior to our client. We look for each time the machine was "down" for service, cleaning, repairs and maintenance- and we look for anomalies, prior deficient breath samples, ambient air, etc., that might undercut the Breath Test results of 0.08% BAC or higher, of our Client. In essence, we try to show that the Breath Test machine was unreliable when our client took the test resulting in the BAC of 0.08%, or higher, being thrown out; and the DUI likely being dismissed as well.

We also obtain the written "Criminal Complaint" from the Clerk of the General District Court that the arresting Police Officer wrote, after our Client's DUI arrest, which is an important summary of the reason for the Traffic DUI stop; an outline of the Field Sobriety Tests given to the client; the PBT Test result; and the BAC Percentage from the police station. We look at every one of these pieces of information as part of the "Jigsaw Puzzle" of our due diligence. We determine if there was "reasonable suspicion" for the police stopping our client; why the client was asked to get out of their vehicle; how many beers or drinks they said they had; how they did on their roadside FST'S and Preliminary Breath Test.

In addition, we have a significant number of immigrants from all over the world in the Northern Virginia area, (many of them are Hispanic, Middle Eastern, Asian, African and Central American) so English is not their first language. Therefore, they often do not understand, and thus can't follow the Police Officer's directions and commands correctly; nor do they always understand the details of doing the Field Sobriety Tests and what they have to do. As part of our due diligence in trying to undercut the Prosecutor's case, we try to show that an immigrant client could not possibly understand or comply with what the police officer wanted them to do -not that they were "drunk" if it appears that they did not do well on the tests, etc.- but, more likely, that they simply could not understand or respond to the officer's commands due to language and cultural reasons.

WHAT IS THE GREATEST NUMBER OF PRIOR DUIS SOMEONE HAS HAD, THAT YOU DEFENDED?

The greatest number of prior DUIs that a person I defended had, before coming to me, was 6 within 10 years. Even someone who went out and got drunk every night of the week, they would probably have a hard time getting pulled over six times in their lifetime; so it is amazing for someone to have 6 DUIs. In my practice, we frequently see people who have had 2 or 3 prior DUIs within a period of 10 years, (the time period in Virginia that prior driving-related convictions are used against a person in court).

In Virginia, a second DUI within 10 years of a person's first DUI conviction results in additional penalties, including a mandatory minimum of 10 days in jail; and if within 5 years, a mandatory minimum of 20 days in jail. Also of note is that in Virginia , a third DUI within 10 years of the first DUI conviction is charged as a Felony, not a Misdemeanor, with the person facing up to five years in prison with a mandatory minimum of 90 days in jail. If two of the prior DUI's occurred within 5 years, there is a mandatory minimum of 6 months in jail.

Are There Any Cases Where The Odds Were Against Your Client But You Prevailed?

Sure, in many, if not most cases. As an example, we had one case where we filed a special written demand for the history of the Breath Test Machine that our client blew into at the Police station, to determine the client's Blood Alcohol Concentration (BAC).

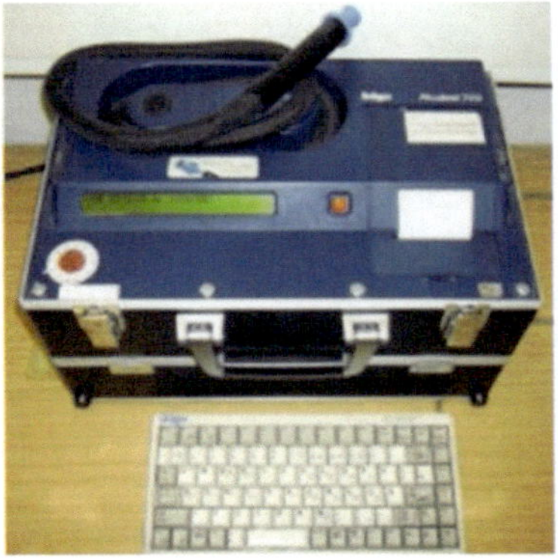

As previously noted, a BAC of 0.08% or higher, is the most incriminating evidence of a DWI. Therefore, being able to keep the BAC Test result of a 0.08%, or higher, out of evidence, will almost always cause a DWI to be dismissed, (though a person can still be convicted of a "DUI" because of the way they looked, drove, acted, walked, talked, smelled of alcohol and performed on the FST's on the road- but it is much more difficult to make the DUI charge stick without a 0.08%, or higher, BAC by a Breath or Blood Test).

Through our written demand of the Breath Test Machine history, we were able to get two months' worth of background information on the Breath Test Machine used in our client's case; and found prior issues and maintenance problems with the Breath Test Machine.

Because of our due diligence in obtaining this critical documentation, we were able to show it to the Commonwealth's Attorney (the Prosecutor) prior to trial; and we were then able to convince the Prosecutor that our clients' extremely high Blood Alcohol Concentration level (BAC) was not reliable and had to be "thrown out".

This meant that the main element in the DWI case against our client, (his very high BAC test result), could not reliably be admitted into evidence, and thus, the Prosecutor had to nolle prosse/dismiss the DWI/DUI charge against our Client.

What Is The Highest BAC You Have Represented For Which You Got A Positive Result?

Someone who has had nothing to drink will blow a BAC of 0.00% BAC. As the person begins drinking, that BAC goes up to 0.01%, 0.02%, 0.03%, up to 0.08% and higher. Driving with a BAC of 0.08% or higher is considered "drunk driving" in Virginia, and nationwide. At this level, a person is considered to be impaired with respect to their judgment and reaction times. The blood alcohol level can continue to rise to 0.09%, 0.10%, 0.11%, and above.

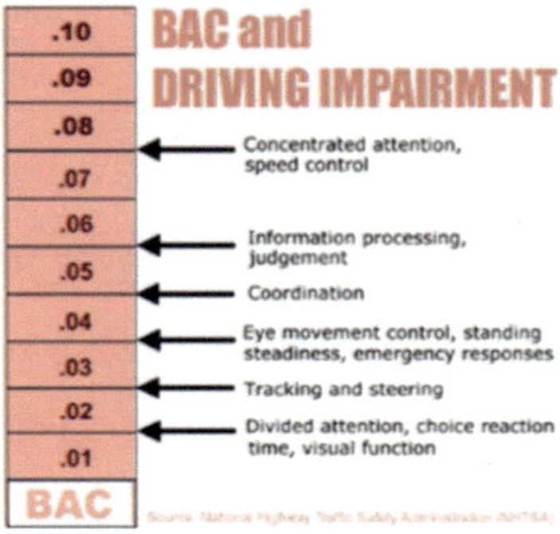

Those people who manage to get to a 0.30% BAC will likely suffer alcohol poisoning and be going into a coma or possibly die if they get to a 0.34% or 0.35% BAC. The highest BAC I have ever defended was a client with a BAC of 0.34%, and I've seen that twice. Both clients were lucky to be alive.

Fortunately, most people's BAC's never gets that high. Most people's BAC falls between the range of a BAC of

0.10%-0.15%, but we have had numerous clients in the 0.15%-0.30% range, and above; yet were still able to get a number of their DUI charges dismissed. And, if not dismissed, we can often get the "BAC number" reduced through a Plea Bargain; and thus get the most severe penalties dramatically reduced or negotiated away.

We do our due diligence and look for the criteria that will allow for a dismissal of the DUI; or, we get the DUI reduced or the punishment reduced, by doing our "homework", and our client doing their "homework"; and looking for "holes" in the prosecution's case. We've worked to get the BAC percentage number dramatically reduced by negotiating with the Prosecutor, so that the person did not get any mandatory jail time that would normally be required when the person has a 0.15% BAC, or more.

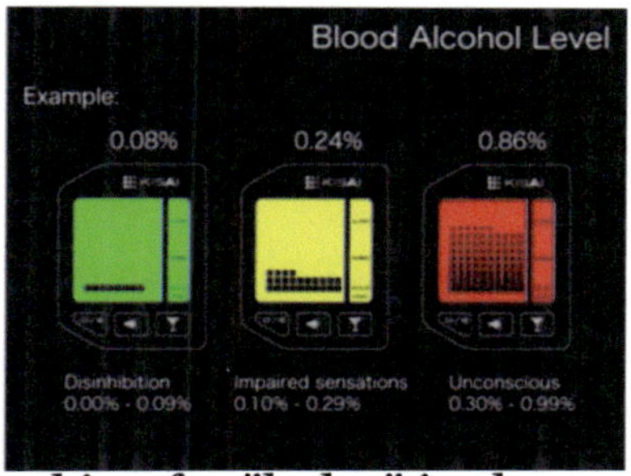

Do People Understand The Implications Of A "Restricted" Driver's License?

No. Most people have no conception of how a "Restricted" License works. They are shocked when they learn that it is mandatory that they lose their driver's license (driving privilege) for an entire year, if they are convicted of a DUI.

They may be able to qualify for a "Restricted" License for the very narrow and strict purposes of only going to and from work, school, doctor appointments, church, school and healthcare for children and elderly parents, etc.; but, they will also have to pay for the installation and rental of an Ignition Interlock system on their primary vehicle for a minimum of six months.

These restrictions, and more, are specific to the "minute". They literally apply exactly to the day and time when you leave your house for these activities, and back; and require that they always take the most direct and shortest route possible between their home and work/ home and school/home and doctors, etc.

People simply do not understand, and cannot grasp, the fact that a "Restricted License" does not even allow them to go to the grocery store, at all; no "quick" stops at 7-11 or McDonalds; no stops to even put gas in their car. That's right! They cannot even get food, medicine, or gas for themselves. How do they get their food, medicine, or gas? The Court simply doesn't care. The law doesn't care. That's their problem to solve for themselves if they get a DUI conviction in Virginia. A person with a "Restricted" License will be arrested if they get pulled over during that year, even if they've just gone off the main road to stop at a gas station, CVS or 7-11.

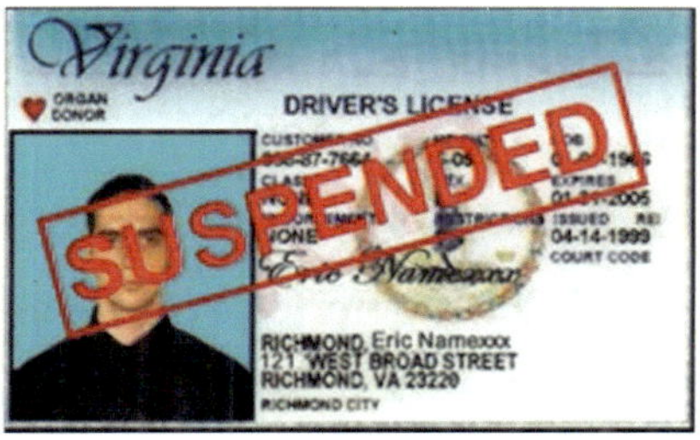

They may have just been pulled over for not using their turn signal, or having a taillight out-but after running their license information through their computer, the Police Officer will see they have a Restricted" License. Then and there they will be arrested, their car will be impounded, and they will be taken to jail and charged with Driving On a Suspended License (also a Class One Misdemeanor punishable by up to one year in jail); as well as facing a "Probation Violation" on their DUI conviction.

If this happens, the person faces not only one year in jail for Driving on Suspended/DUI- Related, but they are facing some or all of the likely suspended jail time that is hanging over their head for one year from the date of conviction of their prior DUI conviction. People don't understand what a "Restricted" License really means; they think it's a "license" to do whatever they want to do; but it's actually a potential "license for failure", hanging over their head for one year

IS IT A "TRAP" FOR SOMEONE TO GET A "RESTRICTED" LICENSE?

Not necessarily, but it can be a trap for some people. I have had clients who did not want to get a "Restricted" License related to a DUI charge because they knew themselves well; and knew that they could not drive within the strict terms of the "Restricted" License rules and restrictions. They knew that they would likely go out and get a beer now and then, even though they are required to be abstinent from all alcohol for one year.

They knew that they would likely violate their "Restricted" License and go to jail with any alcohol on their breath, if ever stopped by the Police-especially when they must blow into their Ignition Interlock device every time they want to start the car- and randomly have to pull their car over when driving, to stop and blow. Frankly, I applaud these people. They know themselves-and they know that they will be setting themselves up for failure with a "Restricted" License.

Most people do want and need a "Restricted" License, and they get it; but their attorney needs to tell them frankly, and in depth, about <u>their</u> responsibilities under a "Restricted" License, so that the client has no doubts or misunderstandings about how, when, and where they can and cannot drive. In my Law Office, when a client qualifies for, and needs a "Restricted" License, we take a significant amount of time to educate them about the terms and conditions of their "Restricted" License... the good and the bad of a "Restricted" License; and how to avoid the bad.

We set them up for success, not failure!

Are There Any "Probation Before Judgment" Or "Diversion Programs" Available For DUI Convictions In Virginia?

No. There are no probation or diversion programs in Virginia for any DUI charge. It is "all or nothing" under Virginia law, which is extremely harsh. There is no "Probation Before Judgment", no "First-Time Offenders" program; no "Diversion Programs"; or anything that will result in an ultimate dismissal of a DUI conviction.

So, the person will either be convicted of the DUI at trial; found not guilty at trial; or, the attorney may be able to negotiate with the Prosecutor to have the DUI charge dismissed or reduced prior to any trial. This said, a recent Virginia Supreme Court decision theoretically allows the Defense Attorney to "request" a Deferred Disposition. But, this is not the statutory law in Virginia.

CAN CRIMINAL CHARGES BE EXPUNGED IN VIRGINIA?

No, and sometimes Yes! There is no expungement available in Virginia for any criminal convictions, including a DUI conviction. If a person pleads guilty, is found guilty, or pleads "no contest" to a DUI charge, then they will have a Permanent Criminal Record for a Class 1 Misdemeanor for the rest of their life. It will greatly hinder, or block their ability to get many jobs; to get a security clearance; to obtain many "licenses"; to successfully apply for many apartment rentals; to get into many colleges; etc.

A person with a DUI conviction will not even be able to be accepted as a volunteer to coach their children's sports leagues at their school, or coach in many organized sports league. Their auto insurance rates will dramatically increase; and the damaging cost to their quality of life will be incalculable. In essence, a DUI conviction will dramatically and negatively affect their life forever, in ways that they cannot even imagine.

This said, if we are able to have their DUI charge "nolle prossed/ dismissed" or they are found “not guilty” at the Trial Court, or on Appeal, without any terms or conditions attached to it, then the client would be eligible to have us file a Petition For Expungement with the Circuit Court. When the Petition/Order To Expunge is granted by the Circuit Court, then the FBI, Homeland Security, Immigration, and all law enforcement, and court systems, nationwide, will be ordered to seal and expunge any history of the DUI charge and arrest record of the Client- effectively enabling the client to go "Back to the future", and never have had a DUI charge in the first place!

What Happens In Accident Cases When The Driver Was Drunk?

We have handled many cases where there was an accident and the person driving had a Blood Alcohol Concentration level of 0.08%, or higher. At first glance, most people would think that the "drunk driver" who had an accident would be in even worse trouble than a "drunk driver" who was routinely stopped by a Police Officer driving down the highway, not in an accident; but had the same Blood Alcohol Concentration level as the "drunk driver" who had an accident.

But, in Virginia, the Prosecutor has to prove three additional elements in a DUI/Accident case beyond what they normally would have to prove in a routine non-accident DUI case, making it much more difficult for the Prosecutor to prove the DUI case.

The Police are almost never at the scene of an accident when it happens. Often, the Police will arrive when the driver is already out of their car. In this case, the Prosecutor will first have to prove that the person was actually the one who was operating the vehicle at the time of the accident. At first, this sounds easy, but often it is not easy for the Prosecutor to actually prove that the person outside the car was the one operating it, if no one has seen them driving at the time of the accident-unless the driver admits to operating the vehicle at the time of the accident.

The second element that the Prosecutor must prove in an accident case is that the person had nothing to drink *after* the accident. At first, most people find this incredible, and inconceivable, but there have been numerous cases, and I have handled many of them, where the driver might actually have had alcohol in the car because they were on their way to/from a party when the accident happened, etc.

Then, they were so upset by the accident that they started drinking the alcohol in their car before the Police arrived; then threw the bottle away. I have handled cases where the driver actually walked home or to a nearby bar because the accident was just a few blocks from their house or a bar. They then had a drink, and came back to the accident scene. This doesn't happen often, but it does happen.

Under Virginia law, the Prosecutor must prove that the driver had nothing to drink between the time of the accident and the time when the Police arrived. It is not the driver's burden to prove that they had nothing to drink after the accident. It is often very difficult for a Prosecutor to prove that this didn't happen, because in most car accidents, there is not anyone else who saw the person after the accident and before the police arrived; and even in multiple car accidents, there is often no one who actually watched the "drunk driver" from the time of the accident until the Police arrived.

The third element that the Prosecutor must prove in an accident case is that the person was arrested within 3 hours of the accident, in order for the Prosecutor to be able to get the person's BAC Breath or Blood Test result admitted into evidence against them. The Prosecutor can virtually always prove what time the person was arrested, because it is noted on the Police Officer's arrest sheets; but proving exactly what time the accident happened is another matter, as there may be no actual evidence to prove it. As you can see, often the Prosecutor cannot prove one or more of these 3 necessary prosecutorial elements that are required to be proven in DUI/Accident Cases, and because of this we have been able to get a number of these type of cases dismissed.

Remember, the prosecution is always required to prove all 3 of these elements:

1) That the driver had nothing to drink after the accident;
2) That the driver was actually behind the wheel at the time of the accident; and,
3) That the driver was arrested within three hours of the accident.

Otherwise, the DUI case will likely be dismissed, or reduced to a much lesser charge.

DISCLAIMER

This publication is intended to be informational only. No legal advice is being given, and no attorney-client relationship is intended to be created by reading this material. If you are facing legal issues, whether criminal or civil, seek professional legal counsel to get your questions answered.

NovaLegalGroup, P.C.

1507 King Street

Alexandria, VA 22314

(703) 548-1462

www.NovaLegalGroup.com

Made in the USA
Monee, IL
05 November 2026

67386569R00038